Starting From Here

Dakota Poetry, Pottery, and Caring

By Jerome W. Freeman

Pottery by Richard Bresnahan

Ex Machina Publishing Company

All photographs in this book courtesy of The Minneapolis Institute of Arts. Used by permission.

"Hospital Reverie" previously appeared in *USD Medicine*, Summer 1996, Vol. XXV, No. 2.

"Holocaust Exhibit and the Dance," "Generations," and "Panic Attack" all appeared previously in *Come and See: Reflections on Values and Caring in Medicine*, by Jerome W. Freeman, published by The Center for Ethics and Caring at Sioux Valley Hospital.

"Generations" was first published in *South Dakota Journal of Medicine*, February 1995 in the essay "Families and Dementia."

Copyright © 1996 by Jerome W. Freeman

Published by Ex Machina Publishing Company
Box 448
Sioux Falls, SD 57101

First Edition, First Printing, December 1996

Mary Freeman and Ron Robinson, editors

Library of Congress Catalog Card Number: 96-61600

ISBN 0-944287-16-6

Printed in United States of America

PINE HILL PRESS, INC.
Freeman, S. Dak. 57029

ii

The author's and the artist's profits from the first printing of this book will be donated to a scholarship program for nursing students at Augustana College, Sioux Falls, S.D., where the art of caring becomes practice.

Starting From Here: First Fire and Caring

The logic of combining poetry and pottery in a volume such as this may require some explanation. On first blush, the two art forms may seem to have more differences than similarities. Both, however, can powerfully reflect human creativity and potential.

In April 1996, an exhibition of Richard Bresnahan's pottery opened at the Minneapolis Institute of Arts. The collection was entitled, "First Fire", as it was comprised of pieces from the initial firing of the nation's largest woodburning kiln at St. John's University. In his remarks at the opening reception, Richard reflected on the connections between pottery and human endeavor. He stressed such concepts as responsibility (exemplified by the sound ecological practices employed at the kiln); the necessity for cooperation and team work among a large number of people during a firing; and the risks and uncertainties that attend the firing of a kiln, especially for the first time. The poem "First Fire," which appears in this volume, reflects upon the emotional tumult and promise of the firing noting "fire like hell, like love, like trust" and describing the resultant pottery as "celebrating creation." Truly, Richard's pottery does champion both our environment and the need to nourish our humanity through cooperation and caring.

Similarly, the poetry in this volume attempts to focus upon caring. It offers portraits of who we are as a people by reflecting upon our relationships to nature and to each other. Much of the poetry looks at illness from the perspective of the patient, the family, or the caregiver. Of all human endeavor, illness care may be paramount in its insistence upon human interaction and sharing. Thus, in a very real sense, the sharing and risk taking of firing a kiln can be a paradigm for the struggles and aspirations which attend illness care. Indeed, the development of the physician/patient relationship, especially in the face of severe illness, is a form of emotional and technical "first fire." Devoted caring greatly nurtures this complex process.

Perhaps these comparisons of pottery and medicine go further than is needed to justify their being combined in this book. Maybe it is enough to note that the economy and simplicity of pottery can resemble the spare verbiage and subtlety of successful poetry. Or perhaps it's enough to say that Richard and I just like the idea of celebrating the creativity, collaboration, and caring that attends our respective disciplines.

Jerome W. Freeman

Table of Contents

Starting From Here: First Fire and Caring iv
Night Vigil 1
Carrying On 3
Stopping at the Farmers' Market 5
Apocalypse 6
If Given the Chance 9
Holocaust Exhibit and the Dance 11
Prairie Runoff 13
In Defense of the Hypochondriac 15
Ten-Year-Old with Rheumatoid Arthritis 17
History Taking 19
Hospital Rounds: A Contemplated Detour . . . 21
Pandora's Box 23
Leaving Grand Rapids 25
Generations 27
Lake Superior in February 29
This Is No Time For Idle Conversation 30
Vision Quest 32
Hospital Reverie 35
flashback 37
Panic Attack 39
First Fire 41
Offsetting Equilibrium 43
Another Elegy 45
Tinnitus 47
DTs 49
Dementia Undone 50
In the Nursing Home 51
Aphasia 53
The Long Splice 55
An Uncertain Flight to Chicago 56
An Altered Allegory 57
Coma Vigil 59
The Price of Genius 60

The Artist's Compromise	61
Still Another Travail	62
lecture on bioethics	63
Medical Transcriptionist	64
Docere	65
Taps	67
To Nana at Ninety-Seven	68
Hallelujah Chorus	69
Huntington's Chorea	71
Chivalry and the Mail	73
Revelations	75
The Old Way	77
The Prairie Gentian	79
In Retrospect	81
The Way Things Are and Are Not	83
sailing together	85
When Wild Turkeys Come Out of the Woods	87
Regrets	89
August Muse	90
The Shunt Poem	91
Reunion	93
Lung Tumor	94
Denouement	95

Index of Photographs

Starting From Here

The Minneapolis Institute of Arts

Night Vigil

The candle of moon
lights our way across
prairie snow.

Snowshoes scrape
echoes of irregular
cadence onto
potent calm.

Deer trails lead
everywhere but
hiding places,

as unseen eyes
take wary measure
of intruders crossing
night's domain.

The Minneapolis Institute of Arts

Carrying On

In an offhand fashion
he sometimes reports
suffering joint pains during
the eighty-eighth year
of getting things done.

When I casually suggest
a trial of some aspirin,
he answers
that lots of folks
use that stuff
as a stick of some kind,
but he never thought
much of it.

He's gnarled and weathered,
making his way through
life and pain with the easy
certainty of someone
on the threshold of heading
somewhere else.

The Minneapolis Institute of Arts

Stopping at the Farmers' Market

Come on over he
says with his arm,
waving a broad arc
toward his pickup.

Bib overalls swell
with the prosperity
of just-picked,
large-kerneled,
best-on-the-lot
sweet corn.

Somehow it doesn't
seem right to walk on by
or offer the excuse
that I'm just waiting
for my wife.

So I take a dozen and
agree with his solemn
pronouncements about
the weather.

Apocalypse

A 26-year-old mother
and wife, four months
relieved of delivery, lies
comatose in the ICU.

Her waiting husband is
cornered and frail, as he
measures my approach
with fear-filled eyes.

I despair of halfhearted
preliminaries and swallow
bile and exhale the truth
that she looks bad, the
dying soon kind.

He and I walk forever
back to her bedside.
Her quiet repose hides
the aneurysm's havoc.
All about keep mostly
thinking there's a mistake
here somewhere.

Three times in the next hour I wash my hands. There is not enough time. This kind of time is never right. All the time, some end lies waiting to happen.

The Minneapolis Institute of Arts

If Given the Chance

Serendipity
is a gift
with strings
attached.

The time to
embrace it is
at the moment
of offering,

as when coming
across a water lily
whose petals
will soon close
for the evening
or forever.

The Minneapolis Institute of Arts

Holocaust Exhibit and the Dance

Footsteps roll echoes along marble floors
of the Landmark Center. I crawl with
fascination and dread through the exhibit,
drawn like the elder Pliny to his volcano.

Photos of somber faces and discarded
bodies and loss of innocence stir up
silent clamor around me. An inscription
on a dull wall asks how these images
can exist. There are no answers here.
A custodian at the exit seems a grim
Charon, measuring my passage
as though hallway was hallowed Styx.

Hearing music, I blankly cross
to the railing. In the lobby below
an assembled crowd concentrates
on eight Polish dancers, swirling joyful
ribbons and tradition before them.

Eerie juxtaposition gives witness
to darkness and second chances.

The Minneapolis Institute of Arts

Prairie Runoff

After rain,
water dances
down quartzite
edges, pausing
in shadowed
places to pray
little eddies,
before joining
the torrent's
fated abandon
toward river
below.

The Minneapolis Institute of Arts

In Defense of the Hypochondriac

It's amazing more bad things
don't happen, since disease
and disaster lurk everywhere.

Possibilities are bad enough,
as you watch for aneurysm,
Alzheimer's and heart attack.
Melanoma may be festering
just below the skin. And
gangrene and impotence
can strike when you least
expect them.

Look at the complacent
dinosaurs who milled about
having things their own way
until they fell into extinction.

Be alert. The worst might
happen. Keep crossing
bridges before you come
to them.

The Minneapolis Institute of Arts

Ten-Year-Old with Rheumatoid Arthritis

Morning begins the battle again
as she lies quietly thinking
of movement. Tentative stretching
immediately laces coils of pain
around each joint, fiercely
locking them into immobility.

It seems better for a time
to let her mind arise effortlessly
from bed and roam about,
making lithe preparation
for the day. She sees herself
twirling across the room
in a dressing ballet, before
descending stairs two
at a time to startle the family
at breakfast routine.

Her musings propel her
to gingerly work elbows and
fingers just enough to sense
the painful ratchet. Catching
her breath, she tries again.

The Minneapolis Institute of Arts

History Taking

Tell me about it in
your own words,
starting from when
the pain began to
seep along cracks
in your confidence.

There can be no
secrets here. What
matters is where
it radiates, filling
your nights with
belief that sorrow
is everywhere.

What matters is
how you grieve
uncertainty and
still dare to hope.

What matters is
where we go
from here.

The Minneapolis Institute of Arts

Hospital Rounds: A Contemplated Detour

As I pass the ICU waiting room,
soft sobbing intrudes on my meditation
of where to go next. Her misery, so
fiercely personal, echoes for me the
corridor tones of all illness vigils.

I muse about a detour to her side
for assurances of solace and hope,
knowing all the while an unbidden
stranger should hardly intrude.

So I'll keep walking on, prepared
to measure different sorrows,
in other places.

The Minneapolis Institute of Arts

Pandora's Box

Pandora shudders visibly
as she leans her weight
across the lid of her dark
casket.

It's not death itself
she fears, so much as
unfettered impulse
waiting to spiral
free.

Soon enough, she knows,
some fate will unleash
her plagues to work their
havoc just beyond her
power to rein them in
again.

The Minneapolis Institute of Arts

Leaving Grand Rapids

Pulling the door closed for the last time,
I shiver in a draft of grandfather's presence.
And recall reading Copperfield together,
both wondering whether we'd become
the heroes of our own lives.

Now memory gives dimensions to
the facade of his history.

His rooms beckon family to ponder
the truth of corners and faith of joists
covered with gentle deeds and lost
opportunities. Windows frame
promises kept and cast light upon
the petty divisions of walls and rules.
The roof acknowledges that style
and proportion can matter,
or not.

What remains for us visitors is what
remains. There are tales here, for
children's children, of sharing shelter
from old storms.

The Minneapolis Institute of Arts

Generations

In this time of imperfect solutions
to your faltering judgment and fierce
desire to maintain independence,
we are all pawns timidly arranged
in battle formation. Often you
speak emotions rather than coherent
thought as you rail against your
children's collusions that have
labeled you as infirm. You angrily
reject repeated explanations as
having never been heard, then turn back
to your conflicts with daily chores,
trusting perhaps that in familiarity
you'll win back your former self.

The Minneapolis Institute of Arts

Lake Superior in February

Ice along shore
creeps out
to dark water
where truth
begins.

Cold secrets churn
under sullen waves.

Imagine walking to
the edge, thinking
it would hold.
There'd be
no

chance to peer in
before being called

to join shipwrecks
still surprised to
be resting on
shrouded
bottom.

This Is No Time For Idle Conversation

Marcel Duchamp,
the champion of
found art, elevated
urinals to a pinnacle
of artistic expression.
To his bold eye,
sturdy curves and
nuances wed form
with function.

As an occasional
student of such
practical elegance,
I prefer undisturbed
focus to insure that
aim is straight and
force sufficient to
credit my efforts.

In such an attitude,
user appreciation
can be impaired
if one's intrepid
neighbor insists
on conversation.

This is no territory
for comment upon
the weather or mere
politics. Such drivel
disrupts concentration
and can stifle flow.
Better that the eyes
are riveted to the
wall and the mind
kept discreetly blank.

The lowly urinal has
earned its place in
modern art, but still
trudges along in the
line of duty bearing
solemn witness to
lavatory etiquette.

Vision Quest

In the old days
the People said
photographs
were spirit
catchers.

A faded image
of Sitting Bull
still summons
quiet dignity
but offers no
clue to secret
thoughts of why
he was standing
still and where
the world was
going.

Today another
ancestor poses
grimly for a chest
picture. Tobacco
stained fingers
fidget as the
processor issues
up a radiograph
with an angry
blemish.

While x-ray
displays tumor,
it reveals too little
of the patient.
The healer must
look beyond
frames frozen in
time and capture
the spirit with
care rather than
images.

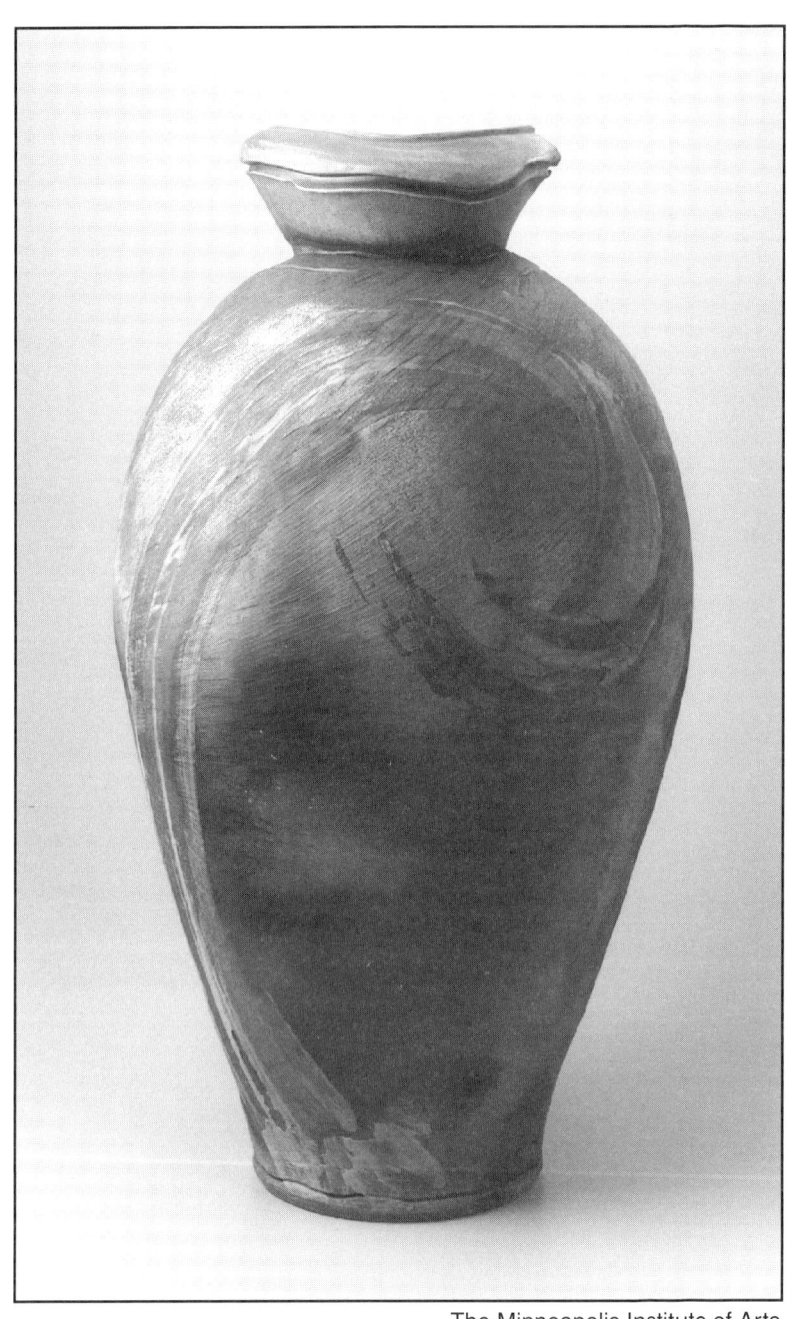

The Minneapolis Institute of Arts

Hospital Reverie

Beyond the window,
crickets and whippoorwills
perform evening song
while the day rewinds itself
around a spool of memory.

From sick bed vantage,
she is mindful of where
she's been and imagines

staying the watch when
there's nothing left to do
but care, and

making a difference in
people's lives most of
the time, and

being given another
chance to get things
right, and

leaving hospital ward
again, restored.

The Minneapolis Institute of Arts

flashback

images of
watergate
recur at
odd times

standing at
a shredding
machine, i
feel vaguely
guilty and
find myself
reciting the
mantra, rose
mary woods

The Minneapolis Institute of Arts

Panic Attack

A wrinkle of foreboding
troubles her brow, then
passes for a time as
she struggles to focus
on calming distractions.

Suddenly, racing heart
and gasping breath and
fear of death trample her
defenses into disarray.

After the tumult, she
trembles in dismay
at harboring such
anarchy.

The Minneapolis Institute of Arts

First Fire
for Richard

In the kiln,
fire like hell
like love like
trust freezes
clay to stone.

Each survivor
is a Phoenix,
cloaked in
earthen hues
and glazed
to celebrate
creation.

The Minneapolis Institute of Arts

Offsetting Equilibrium

Arm over arm the
lift inches upward,
as counterweight
rumbles its descent.

The great wheel
ponderously works
its orbit, while gears
grumble against the
straining cable.

At halfway point
respite is sought.
The elevator pauses,
as if balancing on the
cusp of indecision.

Often in life and
sometimes near death
we are suspended be-
tween possible choices.

To worry the hemp or
life's other decisions into
motion requires firm pull
in the proper direction.

The Minneapolis Institute of Arts

Another Elegy

You'll know who this is for
when I say that three months
is a long time from dying.

Those intruder cells somehow
abandoned their marrow sanctuary,
seeking temporary refuge in other
hidden spaces. His blood count
soared, as a second fleeting lifetime
was composed. And the panorama
of his living and loving was focused
to a locket-sized miniature of such
brilliance that the image will always
illumine your steadfast pride that
once there was this son.

The Minneapolis Institute of Arts

Tinnitus

And still, I am never alone
even in abandoned corridors
or isolated retreats.

The ringing chorus remains
an enduring companion
to any repose.

Bitterly, I've come to know
I'll never hear silence again.

The Minneapolis Institute of Arts

DTs

The mad scramble
of weary caregivers
pauses for breath
about the embattled
bed. All is disarray.

Fierceness has drained
out of him as bulging
vein gulps another
draught of Valium.
Restraints are relieved.

Bugs on the wall creep
away, but he mumbles
salutations to other
demons roving under
closed eyelids.

In fragile days to come,
mere chaos will defer
to remorse and good
intentions. Still, veterans
of such a fray learn never
say never again.

Dementia Undone

Maybe he'll snap out of it
some say, implying that he
might abruptly stand and
dust off his clothes and look
about for a morning paper.
Then, enroute to the coffee shop,
he'd pause to smell lilacs again,
marveling at purple on green
on springtime display.

His grandson, bearing patient
vigil for this resurrection, still
expects to get his hair playfully
mussed again if he waits long
enough.

In the Nursing Home

In dreams you drift
into old age with fair
winds and following
seas, only to awaken
to yesterday's pain on
the morning horizon.

Prospects are limited,
for you are becalmed,
awaiting your rations
of medication and
boredom.

The Minneapolis Institute of Arts

Aphasia

Bitter reign has begun.
His eyes voice silent
reproach, while lips
remain blind.

Mute messages are
posted in his altered
kingdom.

Deference due a
sovereign is easily
lost in a court of
competing voices.

The Minneapolis Institute of Arts

The Long Splice

The splice begins in compromise,
conceding that function does not
require unblemished perfection.

The old order is undone as shy
ends of each rope are unwound
and held together, courting
commitment to new union.

Prior rules are unlayed before
eager strands now woven
together in a new embrace.

Along the way, square knots
are garlands to the ceremony
until modestly disappearing
into the weave.

Stray fibers are clipped before
vernal bond is rolled into shape
in concluding benediction.

Then the conjugal rope is
ready to strain against
forces of separation.

An Uncertain Flight to Chicago

The plane dances to a tune
of turbulence in the rolling
sky before the storm.

We are smaller than life
up here as we hopefully
notch our seatbelts tighter
and grip wobbly armrests
and think of landing back
among the old rules where
gravity pleases to reign
and only birds fly.

An Altered Allegory

"There is a land of the living and a land of the dead and
the bridge is love, the only survival, the only meaning"
from Thorton Wilder, *The Bridge of San Luis Rey*

Uncertain light
at river's edge
waited for faith
to nudge five
travelers into single
file upon the ancient
span.

Each worried the
crossing's sway,
fearing the peril
of careless mis-
step to sudden
destiny.

But none could
sense mean flaws
in construction from
a time of changing
rules and brittle
alliances.

Past compromises
were exposed when
the bridge at San Luis
Rey loosened its grip
and began to slide
downward.

The Minneapolis Institute of Arts

Coma Vigil *

Dawn's bounty spills over
the rim of sky to spread
across darkened
prairie.

Waking comes slowly,
as if an afterthought
to the night business
of getting by.

His problem remains,
as before, saying
goodbye. The morning
drive into town is another
opportunity

to ponder options.
Her choice, if speech
remained, would be
clear. The time has
come.

Shadows still conceal
easy ways of letting
go.

*The term "coma vigil" connotes permanent loss of conscious awareness. It is estimated that over 5000 people in this country exist in such a state.

The Price of Genius

Probably Paganini wouldn't have been surprised to learn he'd be refused burial in sacred ground. The establishment was easily annoyed by his enthusiasms and excesses in superstitious times.

Maybe even he sometimes wondered if his blazing talent was nurtured by a compact with some devil. But mainly, he felt less a musical Faust than fleeing sun, running his ordained orbit with insufficient time.

The Artist's Compromise

Just as maturity begins
to permit a seasoned
perspective of life,
cataracts may blur
the landscape.

Aging Monet painted
through such haze,
melding subjects
together in splashes
of color.

Each canvas challenged
the world to see beauty
in imperfect truth.

Still Another Travail

The canker sore,
that baleful crater,
erodes the gums
without remorse.

Mere food or
drink transforms
smoldering dismay
to painful eruption.

And even when this
Vesuvius renounces
havoc and recedes,
some future turmoil
is foretold.

lecture on bioethics

what i mean to say while
standing podium high is
balance is everything

lament too many
judgments with too
few certainties

proclaim menken right
for knowing that simple
answers to complex
questions are usually
wrong

believe that tumult of
suffering seeks solace
in what is done and
not done

understand the need
to keep trying

Medical Transcriptionist

At the keyboard,
you are mute witness
to a world of secrets,
as you chronicle tales
of unseen lives unfolding
to their destiny.

Docere*

Hippocrates cradled a gentle art
disposed to wither if jealousy
held it to some solitary bosom.
He dispensed healing lore to
callow acolytes eagerly poised
as successors.

Now, in weary light of troubled
days, a descendant mentor stands
in the sway of that tradition while
hazarding new horizons. The call
of illness remains his beacon.
Students are his legacy.

*Doctor is derived from the Latin term *Docere*
meaning "to teach."

The Minneapolis Institute of Arts

Taps
for Brian

Disaster stirred the air
about an eight-year-old,
as his club calf lay bloated
with a belly full of moldy
grain.

Father looked worried,
remarking that the vet might
need to use a knife to tap
the belly.

Unable to await adult time
for getting things done, the
boy quietly withdrew from
the kitchen with butter knife
in hand.

Doing the job himself, he
patiently tapped a childish
rhythm against the distended
abdomen, until the vet made
a solemn entry

in time to watch a mostly
mended calf wobble from
the barn in search of another
pasture.

To Nana at Ninety-Seven

Shrinking into the billows
of your chair, you seem
ready to sink into memory.

Recent frailty is an ill-
disposed anchor dragging
behind you in dark water.
Your works are done.
The ship can sail on
without you now.

Hallelujah Chorus

Seen from some remove,
the conductor seems to
embrace the singers as
her arms sweep an arc
above the festive stage.

Handel's praises stir
celebration that rises
above creed, as pied
chorus summons love
and wonder for this
season and all others.

The Minneapolis Institute of Arts

Huntington's Chorea

Gone is the excess of summer
and sturdy confidence of fall.
Winter prairie is shorn of secrets.
Hints of your family illness,
that disorder, swirl about.

The jerking is dismissed as mere
clumsiness. You do what you do.
Fleeting day drifts into evening, as
more leaves of memory tumble
before a sullen wind.

The Minneapolis Institute of Arts

Chivalry and the Mail

The rural postman answers
regal summons to don a
contrary mantle.

As knight-errant, he is ever
leaning rightward while left
leg stretches diagonally
as if searching some stirrup.

He enters noble conflict
against insufficient tithe
and unplowed snowdrifts
and the carnage of vandals,
while bravely shouldering
the burden of inaccurate
addresses.

Yet acclaim may be muted
even in the presence of
great valor. During heat
of battle, this stalwart
servant is often rudely
overtaken as he inches
along the gravel roads,
patiently tilting at waiting
mailboxes.

The Minneapolis Institute of Arts

Revelations

Piety can be
perilous if too
heavily applied.

Returning from
his seventh grade
religion class
my son noted

that the priest
was so sure of
all answers, you'd
think he had just
shared tea with
God.

The Minneapolis Institute of Arts

The Old Way

Gray profiles of aging wooden elevators tower above the shoulders of scattered towns grown up on Dakota prairie.

The serene giants reign with quiet dignity against the revolving sky. Brusque lines and sharp angles hint at past prosperity, or plans for it, now long abandoned.

Form and prior function make these ancestors more fitting monuments than stone for the way of things out here.

The Minneapolis Institute of Arts

The Prairie Gentian

Every so often, my grandmother
used to say, you get a notion
that life can be grand.

The fall prairie obliges when you
suddenly happen upon crowns
of royal blue crouched here and
there in unassuming brilliance
beneath brazen bluestem waving
before the breeze.

The gentian is like the whisper
of some stirring secret that brings
you up short, blessing your day.

The Minneapolis Institute of Arts

In Retrospect

After aged lichen is stitched to stone,
separation violates an improved order.
A union torn apart is frail and diminished,
as when Arthur watched a fatigued Merlin
leave the room for a final time. Then Camelot
hung in uneasy balance, poised to fall askew.

As indecisive days passed, the king faithfully
recalled the sorcerer's wisdom, but lacked
some instinct for right timing in love and in life.

The Minneapolis Institute of Arts

The Way Things Are and Are Not

Francis says he can't keep up at auctions.
All of a sudden he ends up with something
he may not want or loses it forever.

Courtship can offer similar perplexities.
If pursued to the end, you may roll over
in bed some morning to gaze upon a new
spouse, still a stranger. Or as solitary
alternative, you awaken at night to fitful
dreams of once possible life together
now forfeit.

In either case, there is room for remorse
for what is and might have been.

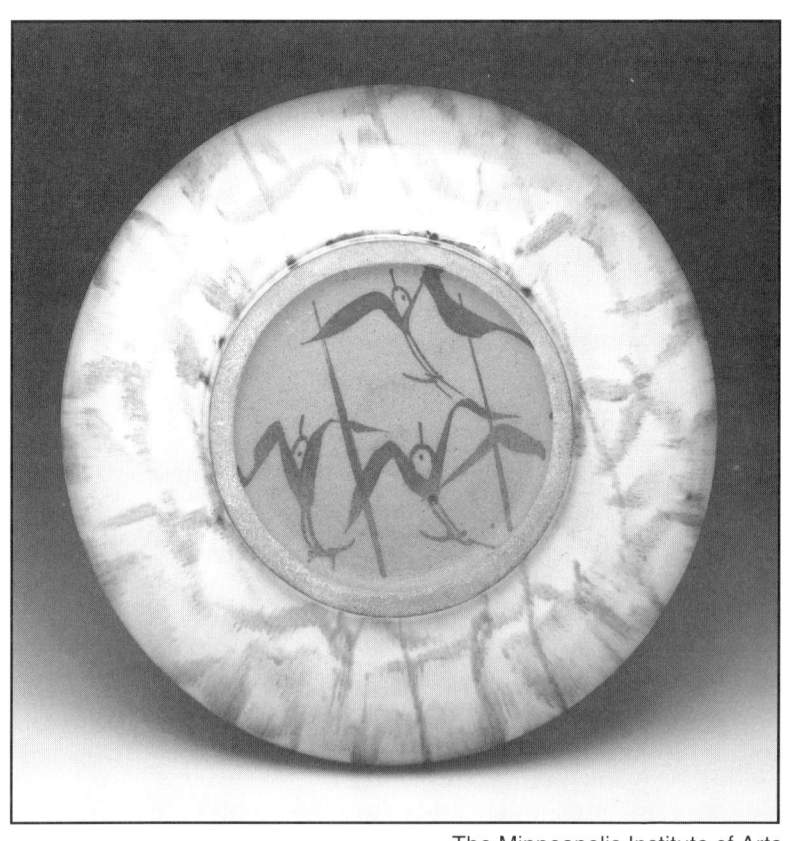

The Minneapolis Institute of Arts

sailing together

imagine that love
is predictable and
calm, a sheltered sea
of languid repose

and contrast that
with the urgency
and turbulence
of learning to roll
in another's waves

The Minneapolis Institute of Arts

When Wild Turkeys Come Out of the Woods

Early mornings they assemble,
thinking turkey thoughts and
gliding through the grass.

The males fan and puff and
waltz around rocks, while
the females studiously ignore
such frippery. They keep
their heads down in search
of breakfast and pray
for abstinence.

The Minneapolis Institute of Arts

Regrets

Before the dawn, as time
falters, memories run like
prairie creeks after rain.

Banks of confidence
erode beneath the torrent,
exposing dormant insecurity
to fading darkness.

Depression, they say,
conjures such early
morning awakenings.

This anxious vigil feels
mostly like opportunity
lost, as when passersby
forgo a chance to speak,

as when promises
are broken.

August Muse

Water gazes back at us
as our wooden boat glides
across the pond to harmony
of sturdy oars.

The world looks different
from out here. Hills are
taller and more reserved,
hinting at secrets.

Occasional trees disperse
sentinel leaves to float over
our reflection like an armada
on patrol.

Birds dart to the surface
and arc away to punctuate
our passage under banner
clouds.

The afternoon waves leisurely
while drifting away.

The Shunt Poem*
for Stacey Jo

The thing about shunts
is they're not perfect.
They are great when
they work, and a pain
in the head when they
don't.

The best shunt is one
you don't think about
for ten years or so.
The second best is one
that gives up making a
ruckus and starts acting
responsibly.

The worst shunt is one
that starts smoking and
hanging out with bacteria.

In truth, you shouldn't be
too hard on shunts. They
work hard and rarely
sleep. Less reliable ones
may get grumpy and
plugged up, but most
keep doing the best
they can.

---

*Some people have problems with the normal flow of brain fluid (hydrocephalus), and require surgical placement of a drainage system (shunt). Such devices, while lifesaving, are unfortunately subject to infections and other malfunctions.

The Minneapolis Institute of Arts

Reunion
*for the class of '66
and all others*

Windswept and worried along
our way, we gather in the lee
to reflect upon our course.

We recall loved ones and
plans that worked and
setting suns now awash

in time's current. And mourn
the loss of other chances,
the certainty of endings.

We long for horizons and
time to look back from
still other isles hidden

on future seas. And plan
to celebrate again who we've
become together and apart.

Lung Tumor

Together, we lost our place when
the doctor said your tests meant
trouble. A sullen growth preyed
upon innocence.

I followed your lead and smiled
when you said things would never
be the same again. As if prediction
was a balm to soothe certainty,
to erase pain before it was written,
to make an ending for what should
never have begun.

In an uncertain future, we avoided
being apart. And gave up cigarettes,
our foil to mere happiness.

Denouement
for a friend

Monarchs are everywhere,
hiding behind leaves and
gliding over the turmoil of
earthbound days that
lack the easy grace of
butterfly symmetry.

When you lost your job
we walked to the park
to find ourselves small
beneath latticed wings
of black on orange,

wrapping us in memory
of dreams and seasons
and migrations for new
beginnings.

Index of Pottery Photographs

The pottery shown in this book is the work of Richard Bresnahan. The photographs are from The Minneapolis Institute of Arts. The titles of the ceramic pieces are listed below.

Temmoku Teabowl, 1995 x
Medium Jar, 1995 2
Platter with Geometric Landscape, 1995 4
Medium Jar, 1995 8
Spice Jars with Lids, 1995 10
Flat-sided Vase, 1995 12
Teabowl, 1995 14
Medium Jar, 1995 16
Platter with Landscape Motif, 1995 18
Foliate-rim Bowl, 1995 20
Spice Jars with Lids, 1995 22
Medium Vase, 1995 24
Teapot, 1995 * 26
Large Jar, 1995 28
Large Jar, 1995 34
Lidded Teapot with 6 lugs, 1995 * 36
Canisters with Lids, 1995 38
Fluted Bowl, 1995 40
Bowl, 1995 42
Teabowl, 1995 44
Large Jar, 1995 46
Teabowl, 1995 48
Teabowl, 1995 52
Pitcher, 1995 54
Fluted Bowl, 1995 58
Teapot, 1995 * 66
Kinuta-shaped Vase, 1995 70
Platter with Horse and Arch, 1995 72
Teabowl, 1995 74
Sake Bottle, 1995 76
Platter with Iris Motif, 1995 78

Pitcher, 1995 80
Cups, 1995 (all three). 82
Bowl with Repeated Bird Motif, 1995 84
Teapot, 1995 * 86
Pitcher, 1995 88
Kinuta-shaped Vase, 1995 92

*These pieces feature knots tied by Paul Krueger.

About the Author

Jerome Freeman, a practicing physician and educator, is on the faculty of the University of South Dakota School of Medicine and Augustana College. He has a particular interest in biomedical ethics and the use of literature for teaching about illness, the patient, and the caregiver. He has published two previous books of poetry, *Something at Last* (1993) and *Easing the Edges* (1994), and a collection of essays, *Come and See* (1995).

About the Artist

Richard Bresnahan is the artist-in-residence at St. John's University where he began the now renowned pottery program in 1979. Prior to that, he studied for four years in Japan where he was recognized as a master potter. His work emphasizes the use of indigenous, renewable materials and reflects the spirit of the North Dakota prairie where he was raised. His recent exhibit at the Minneapolis Institute of Arts is featured in this book.